The Unshakable TRUTH® Journey

GROWTH GUIDES
for Adults

Inspired
Experience the Power of God's Word

JOSH McDOWELL
SEAN McDOWELL

HARVEST HOUSE PUBLISHERS
EUGENE, OREGON

Cover by Koechel Peterson & Associates, Inc., Minneapolis, Minnesota

THE UNSHAKABLE TRUTH is a registered trademark of The Hawkins Children's LLC. Harvest House Publishers, Inc., is the exclusive licensee of the federally registered trademark THE UNSHAKABLE TRUTH.

INSPIRED—EXPERIENCE THE POWER OF GOD'S WORD
Course 2 of The Unshakable Truth® Journey Growth Guides
Copyright © 2011 by Josh McDowell Ministry and Sean McDowell
Published by Harvest House Publishers
Eugene, Oregon 97402
www.harvesthousepublishers.com

ISBN 978-0-7369-3924-9

Printed in the United States of America

11 12 13 14 15 16 17 18 19 / VP-SK / 10 9 8 7 6 5 4 3 2 1

CONTENTS

About the Authors

Authors Josh and Sean McDowell collaborated with their writer to bring you this Unshakable Truth Journey course. The content is based upon Scripture and the McDowells' book *The Unshakable Truth*.®

Over 45-plus years, **Josh McDowell** has spoken to more than 10 million people in 120 countries about the evidence for Christianity and the difference the Christian faith makes in the world. He has authored or coauthored more than 120 books (with more than 51 million copies in print), including such classics as *More Than a Carpenter* and *New Evidence That Demands a Verdict*.

Sean McDowell is an educator and a popular speaker at schools, churches, and conferences nationwide. He is author of *Ethix: Being Bold in a Whatever World*, coauthor of *Understanding Intelligent Design*, and general editor of *Apologetics for a New Generation* and *The Apologetics Study Bible for Students*. He is currently pursuing a PhD in apologetics and worldview studies. Sean's website, www.seanmcdowell.org, offers his blog, many articles and videos, and much additional curriculum.

About the Writer

Dave Bellis is a ministry consultant focusing on ministry planning and product development. He is a writer, producer, and product developer. He and his wife, Becky, have two grown children and live in northeastern Ohio.

Acknowledgments

We would like to thank the many people who brought creativity and insight to forming this course:

Terri Snead and David Ferguson of Great Commandment Network for their writing insights for the TruthTalk and Truth Encounter sections of this study guide.

Terry Glaspey for his insights and guidance as he helped in the development of the Unshakable Truth Journey concept.

Paul Gossard for his skillful editing of this manuscript.

And finally, the entire team at Harvest House, who graciously endured the process with us.

Josh McDowell
Sean McDowell
Dave Bellis

What Is the Unshakable Truth Journey All About?

You hear people talk about having a personal relationship with God and knowing Christ. But what does that really mean? Sure, they probably are saying they are a Christian and God has personally forgiven them of their sins. But is that all of what being a Christian really is—being a person forgiven by God?

We are here to say that being a follower of Christ is much, much more than that. Everything you are and what you are becoming as a person is wrapped up in it. When Jesus said he was "the way, the truth, and the life" (John 14:6) he was offering us a supernatural way to follow in his way, his truth, and his life. As we do, we begin to understand what we were meant to know and be and how we were meant to live. Actually, when we become a follower of Christ we begin to take on Jesus' view of the world and begin to think like and be motivated like and live like Christ. And that brings incredible joy and satisfaction to life.

So when we see life and relationships as Jesus sees them, we begin to get a clear picture of who we are and discover our true identity. We begin to realize why we are here and recognize our purpose and meaning in life. We begin to know where we are going and experience our destiny and mission in a life larger than ourselves. Being a Christian—a committed follower of Christ—unlocks our identity, purpose, and destiny in life. It is then that the natural process of spiritual reproduction takes place. That is when imparting the faith to our family and others around us becomes a reality. But what is involved in being that kind of a follower of Christ—a person who has joy and satisfaction in life and knows how to effectively impart the faith to the next generation?

The Unshakable Truth Journey gets to the core of what being a true follower of Christ means and what knowing Christ is all about. Together you and your group will begin a journey that will last a lifetime. It is a journey into what you as a follower of Christ are to believe biblically, how you process your beliefs into core values, and how you live them out in all your relationships. In fact, we will take the core truths of Christianity and break them down into a five-step process:

1. ***What truths do you as a Christian believe biblically?***

   In the first step you and your group will interact

with what we as Christians believe about God, his Word, and so on.

2. **Why do you believe those truths?**

Sure, you can say you believe certain truths because they are biblical, but when you know *why* they are true it grounds you in your faith. Additionally, it gives you confidence to pass them on to others—especially your family.

3. **How are these truths relevant to life?**

In many respects truth isn't very meaningful until you see how it is relevant to your own life.

4. **How do you live these truths out personally?**

Knowing how the truth of Christianity is relevant is necessary, but what it leads to is understanding how that truth is to become a living reality in your own life. That's where the rubber meets the road, so to speak.

5. **How do you, as a group, live these truths out before your community and world?**

As Christians we are all to be "salt" and "light" to the world around us. In this step you and your group will discover how to impact your own community with truth that is lived out corporately—as a body.

Be warned! The Unshakable Truth Journey isn't a program to study what Christianity is all about. Simply discovering what something is about has great limitations and ends up being of little value. Rather, this journey is about experiencing firsthand how God's truth is to be experienced in your life right now and, in fact, for the rest of your life. It's about knowing God's truth in a real, experiential way. The apostle John said, "It is by our actions that we know we are living in the truth" (1 John 3:19). You will be challenged repeatedly to increasingly know certain truths by experiencing them continually in your relationship with God and with those around you. It is then you will be able to pass on this ever-increasing faith journey to your family and friends.

There will be two specific exercises that appear throughout these courses. The first is entitled "Truth Encounter." This section is an invitation for you to stop and carefully reflect on the truth of each session. You'll be asked to encounter a truth of God as you relate personally with Jesus, as you live out the truth of God's Word with your small group, or as you relate personally with his people. Please don't rush past these Truth Encounters. They are designed to equip you in how to experience truth right in the room you're in!

The second exercise is an assignment for the week, called

"TruthTalk." The TruthTalks are designed as conversation start-ers—ways to engage others in spiritual discussions. They will create opportunities for you to share what you've experienced in this course with others around you. This will help you com-municate God's truth with others as you share vulnerably about your own Unshakable Truth Journey.

What you discover here is to last a lifetime and beyond because God's truths are designed to be enjoyed forever. You see, expe-riencing God's truth and knowing him will grow throughout eternity, and your love of him will expand to contain it. And that process begins in the here and now. Your relationship with God may have begun 5 months, 5 years, or 50 years ago—it doesn't matter. The truths explored in these courses are to be applied at every level of life. And what is so encouraging is that while these truths are eternally deep they can be embraced and experienced by even a young child. That is the beauty and mystery of God's truth!

This particular Unshakable Truth Journey is one of 12 different courses, all of which are based upon Josh and Sean McDow-ell's book *The Unshakable Truth*. That is the companion book to this course. The book covers 12 core truths of the Christian faith. The growth guide you have in your hand covers the truth about God and his Word: the Bible. God *spoke*—he gave us his Word for a very clear purpose. Together we will explore how his Word provides for us and protects us. These five sessions lay the foundation for how we are to live a life of fulfillment. Check out the other Unshakable Truth courses in the appendix of this growth guide.

Okay then, let our journey begin.

WHAT WE BELIEVE ABOUT GOD'S WORD

The Bible is the most widely distributed book in all of history. Originally written in Hebrew, Greek, and Aramaic, it has now been translated into more than 2400 languages, which means that over 90 percent of the world's population has it available in their primary language!

But what is the Bible? How would you describe what it is and what it does?

_____

_____

_____

_____

OUR GROUP OBJECTIVE

To develop a deeper appreciation for God's Word and praise him for wanting us to know him as he is.

Someone read 2 Timothy 3:16-17.

Based on this passage, is the Bible a set of guidelines to follow in order to live right? Why or why not?

_____

_____

_____

_____

A recent study among professed Christians revealed that 81 percent said the essence of the Christian faith was "trying harder to follow the rules described in the Bible." Do you personally agree with that assessment? _____

Have you ever written to a person you loved—say, in a dating relationship? You may have written love letters to your spouse prior to marriage. What do love letters attempt to do? Why are they written? What are they trying to accomplish?

_____

_____

_____

_____

Communication in some form or another is necessary for an intimate relationship to deepen. But communications such as written letters or e-mails are not an end in themselves; they are a *means* to an end. The end is a deepened love relationship.

Someone read Psalm 19:7-9 and list here the six things the law, commands, precepts, and respect/fear of the law actually are.

_____, _____, _____,

_____, _____, _____.

Are any of these qualities or characteristics of the law reflective of the author, God? If so, which ones?

_____

_____

So what is God's motive or reason for giving us his Word? Someone first read John 17:3.

_____

_____

_____

_____

Someone read the following aloud. (This is drawn from chapter 8 of *The Unshakable Truth* book.)

When God gave us his Word, he in effect was saying, "Devote yourself to knowing me intimately, and open yourself to me fully so my ways will become your ways." God's design of humans is such that an intimate relationship with him is the only way they can succeed in living meaningful lives of joy. Moses understood this, and he begged God, "If you are pleased with me, teach me your ways so I may know you" (Exodus 33:13 NIV). Following God's ways leads to knowing him; knowing him leads to being and living like him; being and living like him leads to joy.

In other words, when we demonstrate our love for God by acting according to his ways, we enjoy blessing because God's ways reflect who he is—the ultimate good and perfect God. The closer we come to living like him, the closer we come to goodness and perfection. Being honest, for example, brings blessing because God is true. Staying sexually pure brings blessing because God is holy. Treating others justly brings blessing because God is just.

God's commands and instructions to act in certain ways flow out of who he is and how he himself acts. When we seek to know him intimately—love him—we can take on his ways and reap the benefits.

Thus, we can say the Bible is a perfectly right set of laws and guidelines that flow out of a perfectly right God to instruct us to live as God designed us to live. Therefore:

> **We believe the truth that the Bible is God's revelation of himself to us, which declares his ways for us to follow.**

It is the revelation of "a God who is passionate about his relationship with you" (Exodus 34:14). And it is a revelation that—from the first words Moses penned in the book of Genesis to the last word John wrote in Revelation—reflects the loving heart of a God who wants us to be in right relationship with him so we can enjoy all the benefits that relationship offers.

To sum it up: Scripture is the means by which God has chosen to introduce and reveal himself to you so he can enjoy a relationship with you. God's Word—the record of all his ways—is given to you for a relational purpose: so you may know him and enjoy all the blessings of a relationship with your loving Creator.

King David understood that his meaning in life would be realized as he longed after God and followed in his ways. Someone read Psalm 25:4-10.

Identify the things that David was reaching for and wanting from God, such as "a path where he should walk," "a right road to follow," and so on.

_____

_____

_____

_____

Identify the characteristics of the God David wanted to know, such as "the God who saves me," "the God of unfailing love and compassion," and so on.

_____

_____

_____

_____

Truth Encounter

Someone read John 20:30-31.

Jesus miraculously appeared to his followers after his

resurrection. And the apostles wrote down what Jesus did and said. Why?

_____

_____

_____

_____

The apostle John reminds us that we not only have a God who wants us to know and believe the truths of his Word, but we have a God who offers deep closeness and personal relationship. We not only have a God who has provided a written record of the truth of his Son and his provision for eternal life—we have a God who deeply desires for us to have living fellowship with him now! God's written Word enables us to know him personally and live life in intimacy with him at this very moment.

Someone read Psalm 119:162.

Take time now to rejoice in God's giving us his Word. What does your rejoicing sound like?

For example: "I am glad for God's instructions because _____

_____

_____

_____."

"I am glad for God's revealing of his nature and character because

_____

_____

_____."

"I am humbled and rejoice that God wants me to be his friend
because _____

_____

_____."

Other expressions of rejoicing in his Word are _____

_____

_____

_____

Consider singing songs of praise and worship to God.

Does It Matter If It's Reliable or Not?

How many commandments did God give to Moses on Mt.
Sinai? _____ Are you sure? What if God actually gave
Moses 12 commandments, and those who copied the Old Testament manuscripts left two out many years later? What problem
or consequence does that pose for us as Christians?

_____

_____

_____

_____

What if a hundred years after Jesus gave the Sermon on the Mount, a scribe copying the Scriptures put his own twist on what Jesus said, which actually changed the meaning of Jesus' words? That would mean we wouldn't have the accurate teachings of Jesus. Would that pose a problem? Why or why not?

_____

_____

_____

_____

Someone read Deuteronomy 10:12-13 and 11:26.

These words were given to the Children of Israel. But do they also apply to us? How does disobeying the words of God bring pain and heartache to a life today? Give an example.

_____

_____

_____

_____

Let's say the facts and events of the Bible weren't carefully and truthfully recorded and passed down to us. Would we still suffer consequences for failing to follow in God's ways even though it wasn't our fault, even though we didn't know? Why or why not?

_____

_____

_____

_____

Someone read the following drawn from chapter 8 of *The Unshakable Truth* book.

> Knowing God, living in relationship with him, and enjoying the protection and provision of his Word are dependent on our receiving and possessing an accurate revelation of him. Unless the Bible is reliable, we have no assurance that its teachings we follow and obey are true at all. Imagine, for example, that God really did give Moses 12 commandments, and some scribe along the way decided to eliminate two of them. We would—at best—possess an incomplete picture of what God is like and what he requires of us. And at worst we would be courting disaster, inviting "curses, confusion, and disillusionment in everything [we] do" (Deuteronomy 28:20).
>
> If we hope to enjoy the benefits of knowing God for who he really is, we must be sure that we have a Bible that accurately represents what he inspired people to write on his behalf. Because if his Word was not accurately recorded and relayed to us, then we and our children, like the nation of Israel, will be cheated in our efforts to know him and may be exposed to "curses, confusion, and disillusionment."

Don't worry—God's Word is reliable!

Someone read what Jesus said in Matthew 5:18 and Matthew 24:35. What is Jesus assuring us of, and how can he be so sure?

_____

_____

_____

_____

Is it okay to have some doubts or questions about the reliability of the Bible? Why or why not?

_____

_____

_____

_____

God has miraculously preserved his Word down through the ages so we can have an accurate reflection of what he inspired men to write. And when we see the clear evidence of that, we don't have to doubt or be concerned for a moment. In the next session we will cover how we can know beyond a shadow of a doubt that the Bible is reliable.

TruthTalk—An Assignment of the Week

This week, share with a family member or friend about the relational Bible from a relational God who wants you to know him. Consider saying something like:

The revelations of God have been recorded in written form and preserved in the pages of Scripture. But if the facts and events of the Bible weren't carefully and truthfully recorded, then the Bible we have today is a distorted reflection of God's nature and character. So knowing God and living in relationship with him are dependent on our receiving the

1 "I've been learning some things in my group about God's Word. At times, I've thought that the Bible was only a book of important beliefs or things to do. I now know that God's Word was written for so much more. I'm so grateful God wrote the Bible so I could have a relationship with him. That's been true for me lately because…

_____

_____

_____

_____

_____."

2 "I've recently come to know God in a more personal way by reading revelations and possessing an accurate revelation of him. Unless the Bible is reliable, we have no assurance that its teachings we obey and follow are true at all.

the Bible. I've come to know and love him for his…

_____

_____

_____

_____

_____."

3 "I love reading the Bible because it helps me know God more. I've been especially glad to know that he…

_____

_____

_____

_____

_____."

Read chapter 9 of *The Unshakable Truth* book.

HOW DO WE KNOW THE BIBLE IS RELIABLE?

Review: How did your TruthTalk assignment go this week? What was the response?

_____

_____

_____

_____

Before the revolutionary improvements in printing in the 1400s, how were nearly all historical documents and literature passed down?

_____

_____

_____

_____

How could a generation, say in 50 BC, be sure a writing from 100 BC had been accurately recorded? Wasn't a handwritten system of passing on historical information bound to be flawed? It often depended upon someone eventually writing down what they heard other people say about an event that might have happened 20 or 30 years prior. With such a system, how can we be sure we have an accurate account of, for instance, what Jesus said?

_____

_____

_____

OUR GROUP OBJECTIVE

To gain a greater understanding of why we can trust the Bible to be a reliable revelation of God and a deeper sense of gratitude for what the Bible means to us.

Someone read Luke 1:1-4.

What distinguished Luke's writing of the accounts of Jesus? What source material did he use?

_____

_____

_____

_____

One or more people read John 19:35; 1 John 1:3; and 2 Peter 1:16.

Where did these writers of Scripture get their information?

_____

_____

_____

_____

Someone read the following drawn from chapter 8 of *The Unshakable Truth*.

> God could have spoken through anyone, from anywhere, to write his words about Christ. But to give us additional confidence in the truth, he worked through eyewitnesses of those who walked with Jesus, ate with him, and lived their lives with him. And whom did he choose as his most prolific writer? The apostle Paul, whose dramatic conversion from persecutor of Christians to planter of churches made him perhaps the most credible witness of all!
>
> Those through whom he transmitted his inspired Word were also apostles. These men could rely on their own eyewitness experiences, and they could appeal to the firsthand knowledge of their

contemporaries, even their most severe opponents (see Acts 2:32; 3:15; 13:31; 1 Corinthians 15:3-8). They not only said, "Look, we saw this," or "We heard that," but they were also so confident in what they wrote as to say, in effect, "Check it out," "Ask around," and "You know it as well as I do!" Such challenges demonstrate a supreme confidence that the "God-breathed" Word was recorded exactly as God spoke it (2 Timothy 3:16 NIV).

Such careful inspiration and supervision of the Bible underlines God's purpose, that not a single piece of this revelation about himself or the human condition be left to chance or recorded incorrectly. Ample evidence exists to suggest that he was very selective in the people he chose to record his words. They were people who for the most part had first-hand knowledge of key events and who were credible channels to record exactly those truths he wanted us to know.

The Case of the Meticulous Scribes

Someone read the following drawn from chapter 8 of *The Unshakable Truth*.

Hand-copying of the Old Testament was the responsibility of a group of men who were trained as skilled scribes and gave their lives to writing. For many years before and after the time of Jesus it was their responsibility to copy Scripture. These particular scribes, some known as Masoretic scribes, devoted themselves to making sure that the Holy Scriptures were copied letter for letter, word for word. Their rules for copying Scripture were so strict that when a copy was made it was considered to be an exact duplicate, just as if you had made it from a copy machine. When a copy was finished it was called a manuscript.

A scribe would begin his day of transcribing a manuscript by ceremonially washing his entire body. He would then robe himself in full Jewish dress before sitting down at his desk. As he wrote, if he came to the Hebrew name of God, he could not begin writing the name with a pen newly dipped in ink for fear it would smear the page. Once he began writing the name of God, he could not stop or allow himself to be distracted…even if a king were to enter the room. The scribe was obligated to continue without interruption until he finished penning the holy name of the one true God.

The Masoretic guidelines for copying manuscripts also required that…

- the scroll be written on the skin of a clean animal.

- each skin contain a specified number of columns, equal throughout the entire book.

- the length of each column extend no less than 48 lines and no more than 60.

- the column breadth consist of exactly 30 letters.

- the space of a thread appear between every consonant.

- the breadth of nine consonants be inserted between each section.

- a space of three lines appear between each book.

- the fifth book of Moses (Deuteronomy) conclude exactly with a full line.

- nothing—not even the shortest word—be copied from memory, but rather be copied letter by letter.

- the scribe count the number of times each letter of the alphabet occurred in each book and compare it to the original.

- if a manuscript was found to contain over three mistakes, it be discarded.

Why do you suppose God instilled in the Masoretes such a

painstaking reverence for the Hebrew Scriptures? Why is God
interested in your receiving an accurate Scripture?

_____

_____

_____

_____

||||||||||||||||||||||||||||||||||||||||||||||||||||||||||||||||||||||||||||||||||||||||||||||||||||

But What About the Accuracy of the New Testament?

The Hebrew scribes did not copy the manuscripts of the New
Testament. So God did a new thing to ensure that the words of
Jesus and his followers would be preserved accurately for us.

To tell if ancient manuscripts are reliable we 1) measure the time
between the original writing and the first manuscript copy; and
2) determine how many manuscript copies are still in existence.
The shorter the time between the original writing and the first
copy and the more manuscripts there are, the more accurate
the manuscripts are considered.

For example, virtually everything we know today about Julius
Caesar's campaigns in Gaul (present-day France) comes from
ten manuscript copies of *The Gallic Wars*, the earliest of which
dates to just within 1000 years of the time it was originally written. The most reliable writing in secular history is Homer's *Iliad*,

with 643 manuscripts, the earliest of which dates to within 400 years of the original writing.

Let's look at this chart of classical literature.

Author	Book	Date written	Date of earliest existing copies	Time gap	Number of copies
Homer	*Iliad*	800 BC	c. 400 BC	c. 400 years	643
Herodotus	*History*	480–425 BC	c. AD 900	c. 1350 years	8
Thucydides	*History*	460–400 BC	AD 900	c. 1300 years	8
Plato		400 BC	c. AD 900	c. 1300 years	7
Demosthenes		300 BC	c. AD 1100	c. 1400 years	200
Caesar	*Gallic Wars*	100–44 BC	c. AD 900	c. 1000 years	10
Livy	*History of Rome*	59 BC-AD 17	fourth century (partial); mostly tenth century	c. 400 years c. 1000 years	1 partial 19 complete
Tacitus	*Annals*	AD 100	c. AD 1100	c. 1000 years	20
Pliny Secundus	*Natural History*	AD 61–113	c. AD 850	c. 750 years	7

||||||||||||||||||||||||||||||||||||||||||||||||||||||||||||||||||||||||||||||||||||||||

The New Testament has no equal

Using this accepted standard for evaluating the reliability of ancient writings, the New Testament stands alone. It has no equal. No other book of the ancient world can even compare to its reliability. Take a look at this chart:

Author	Book	Date of earliest existing copies	Time gap	Number of copies
John	New Testament	c. AD 130	50-plus years	Fragments
The rest of the New Testament books		c. AD 200 (books)	100 years	
		c. AD 250 (most of New Testament)	150 years	
		c. AD 325 (complete New Testament)	225 years	5600-plus Greek manuscripts
		c. AD 366–384 (Latin Vulgate translation)	284 years	
		c. AD 400–500 (other translations)	400 years	19,000-plus translated manuscripts
		TOTALS	50–400 years	24,900-plus manuscripts

There are nearly 25,000 manuscripts or fragments of manuscripts, with some dating back to within 50 years of the original writings. And none are more than 400 years more recent than the originals. Incredible!

||||||||||||||||||||||||||||||||||||||||||||||||||||||||||||||||||||||||||||||||||||

Understanding God's Accurate Revelation

When you hold a Bible in your hand you can be sure it is the most accurate and reliable writing in all of history! God wanted you to be sure that the Bible you read is an accurate revelation of himself to you. He wants you to know him for who he really is.

So can anyone simply pick up a Bible, read it, and come to know God? Why or why not?

_____

_____

_____

_____

Someone read 1 Corinthians 2:11-16.

Who reveals the truths of God to us, and why can't non-Christians understand them?

_____

_____

_____

_____

With an accurate Bible and the Holy Spirit to guide you, can you or anyone sit down without the aid of others and unlock all the truths of God? Why or why not?

_____

_____

_____

_____

Someone read 2 Timothy 2:14-15.

Why do we need others in the body of Christ (his church) to help us understand who God is, his truth, and how to live it out?

_____

_____

_____

_____

Someone read the following from *The Unshakable Truth*.

> Having an accurate Bible and the presence of the Holy Spirit in our lives does not mean pastors and teachers of the Word are not necessary. Nor does it mean we are not to study God's Word diligently. We must not simply disregard all study or the wisdom of good teachers and rely solely on the internal leading of the Spirit. Because we are fallen, our perception is often dim and foggy, and we are subject to being fooled by voices that we think may be from God but are actually from darker sources. Paul warned the church at Corinth of false teachers who "have fooled you by disguising themselves as apostles of Christ. But I am not surprised! Even Satan can disguise himself as an angel of light" (2 Corinthians 11:13-14).
>
> If we rely solely on internal proddings that we think are from the Holy Spirit, we make ourselves vulnerable to this kind of deception. That is why

we must continually check our internal impulses by the Bible and by the wisdom of godly teachers. These sources provide a crosscheck to assure us that the internal guidance we receive is indeed from God's Holy Spirit. God will not contradict himself in his Word. What the Holy Spirit impels us to do will be consistent with what we find in the Bible. God involves the wise and godly teachings of men and women around us to lead us into all truth. The Holy Spirit is there to superintend in our own study and the godly teachings of others to open our hearts and minds to him and his truth.

 ‖‖‖

Truth Encounter

At times, some of us may have seen the Bible as a list of beliefs to proclaim or commands to follow. But doesn't it make more sense that God would carefully preserve his written Word so we would have an accurate reflection of who he is in order that we might come to understand and know and love him, the One who wrote it? When we consider how much God worked to carefully preserve the accuracy of his Word, we see his commitment to relationship.

Someone read 2 Timothy 3:16-17.

This passage says that God's Word is useful to do what?

_____

_____

_____

_____

_____

_____

_____

Why would God give us his Word for those reasons?

_____

_____

_____

_____

Have you at times viewed God's Word as a book of to-do lists?
What does that tell you about your view of its author?

_____

_____

_____

_____

Share together how you want to view God's Word as his means
to share his heart of love to you. What steps can you take as a
group to maintain that perspective?

_____

_____

_____

_____

Share your hearts with God in prayer. Tell him how you want to view his Word. Praise him for giving you his heart of love and loving instructions through his Word.

_____

_____

_____

_____

TruthTalk—An Assignment of the Week

Take time this week to share with a family member or friend what you have discovered about God's Word in this session. Consider saying something like:

1 "I know there are some people who have a hard time believing that the Bible is true because they are not convinced of its accuracy. I've learned the process by which

The careful inspiration and supervision of the Bible underlines God's purpose, that not a single piece of this revelation about himself or the human condition be left to chance or recorded incorrectly. Ample evidence exists to suggest that God was very selective in the people he chose to record his words—people who for the most part had firsthand knowledge of key events and who were credible channels to record exactly those truths he wanted us to know.

the Bible was preserved, and it's helped me feel secure about what I believe. Here is some of what I discovered:

_____

_____

_____

_____."

2 "I know it may be hard to believe that the Bible is true. There may even be some people who claim that the Bible isn't true because of its inaccuracies. I've recently learned the process by which the Bible was carefully preserved—for example, in such areas as…

_____

_____

_____

_____.

"Is there a good time when I can tell you more about what I've learned?"

3 "I now 'get' why God worked so hard to protect the Bible and make sure it was written and translated exactly the way he intended: He wanted the Bible protected so that we could be secure it was the real thing. And because we know it's the real thing, we can rest assured of how important it was to God that we be able to read of his love for us. That's been especially important to me because…

_____

_____

_____

_____."

Read chapter 10 of *The Unshakable Truth* book.

WHY FOLLOWING GOD'S WAYS IS FOR OUR GOOD

Review: How did your TruthTalk assignment go this week? What was the response?

_____

_____

_____

_____

When you were growing up, did you ever ask "why" when one of your parents told you to do something? How did your parents respond to your "why" question?

_____

_____

_____

_____

Has one of your children asked "why" when you gave him or her a specific instruction? How did you respond to "why" when your child asked it?

_____

_____

_____

_____

We all want our children to obey without needing a reason for every instruction we give, but it is healthy to know why certain behaviors are right and why they are wrong, especially when it comes to specific behaviors and moral truth.

OUR GROUP OBJECTIVE

To discover why God is the definer of moral truth and how our obedience to him protects us and provides for us.

The Bottom-Line Answer to "Why"

Have at least two people in your group answer these questions aloud.

Do you believe sexual immorality (premarital and extramarital sex) is wrong? _____

If you believe it is wrong, *why* do you believe it is wrong?

_____

_____

_____

_____

Why? For example, if you believe immorality is wrong because your parents or church taught it was wrong, then why did they say it was wrong? Or, if you believe it is wrong because the Bible said it was wrong, then why does the Bible teach it is wrong?

_____

_____

_____

_____

Even if you answer that God commands us to be sexually moral, then *why* does God command it?

_____

_____

_____

_____

Some would say that sexual immorality or any sinful behavior is wrong simply because God says it's wrong. Is that really the bottom-line answer? Why or why not?

_____

_____

_____

_____

Someone read Hebrews 4:12 and 2 Timothy 3:16.

What do these Scripture passages indicate? Are they saying that God's Word is the bottom line for defining what is right or wrong? Why or why not?

_____

_____

_____

_____

Someone read Hebrews 4:12 again and then verse 13.

Verse 12 indicates that the Word of God judges our behavior and exposes us for who we are. What insight does verse 13 add to verse 12? To whom are we exposed?

_____

_____

_____

_____

Someone read the following.

> It may sound shocking to some people to say that the Bible with its commands and rules does not ultimately define truth—moral right and wrong. There is no authority or power in the words of

Scripture in and of themselves. The authority and power of Scripture is derived from the author of the Book—God himself. When the Hebrew writer said, "The word of God is full of living power," and "it exposes us for what we really are" (Hebrews 4:12), he quickly added, "Nothing in all creation can hide from him…This is the God to whom we must explain all that we have done" (verse 13). Scripture is telling us that the very person of God defines moral truth and is behind the power and authority of the Book.

So why is all sin wrong? Because it violates the very person and nature of God himself. God says sin is wrong because it is contrary to the very essence of him who is righteous and good.

The reason lying, stealing, and fraud are wrong and honesty is right is because God is true. (See Deuteronomy 32:4; Titus 1:2; Romans 3:4.)

The reason chastity is moral and promiscuity is immoral is because God is pure and faithful. (See 1 John 3:3; Deuteronomy 7:9; 2 Timothy 2:13.)

The reason love is a virtue and hatred is a vice is because God is love. (See 1 John 4:16; Jeremiah 31:3.)

The reason vengeance is wrong and mercy is right is that God by nature is mercy. (See Micah 7:18; 1 Kings 3:6; Psalm 107:1.)

God's person and character define all that is perfect, right, good, and blessed. "Whatever is good and perfect," the writer of the book of James says, "comes to us from God above" (James 1:17). So when we act according to God's truth (obeying his Word) we enjoy blessing (protection and provision) because God's ways reflect his absolute goodness.

Truth—moral right and wrong—is therefore defined by _____, because he is the essence of all that is righteous and holy and good.

||||||||||||||||||||||||||||||||||||||||||||||||||||||||||||||||||||||||||||||||||||||||

Finish these sentences:

We are protected from harm and provided with blessing when we live _____

_____

_____ .

We suffer negative consequences when we fail to _____

_____

_____ .

Someone read Genesis 1:27.

Discuss an example of what living in God's image and following in his ways looks like and how that brings protection and provision in our lives.

_____

_____

_____

_____

_____

_____

_____

||||||||||||||||||||||||||||||||||||||||||||||||||||||||||||||||||||||||||||||||||||||||||||||

Objective vs. Subjective Truth

Truth—moral right and wrong—is defined by God. But is it universal—that is, does it define right and wrong for everyone? Why or why not?

_____

_____

_____

_____

You have probably heard it said, "It may be wrong for you, but it's not necessarily wrong for me" or "I have to choose for myself what's right for me." Where does this thinking come from? Why is it such a widely held view?

_____

_____

_____

_____

Someone read the following and discuss which model of truth you sense your children or their friends (this generation) accept as theirs. This is drawn from chapter 10 of *The Unshakable Truth*.

> In our culture there are two distinct models for knowing that something is true. Each model affects how we see and apply God's Word. The two models actually represent two radically different and opposing worldviews.
>
> - *Model #1:* Truth is defined by God for everyone; it is objective and universal. The truth is known through discovering God and his Word.
>
> - *Model #2:* What is true is defined by the individual; it is subjective and situational. Truth is known through simply choosing to believe it.
>
> The first model acknowledges that God—not humans—is central, that he is the source of all things, and that he rules over all. God is the repository of truth, the author and judge of all that is right and wrong.
>
> The second model, on the other hand, places the individual in control of moral matters. Because the

standard resides within the individual, it is particular to that specific person (subjective) and circumstance (situational). In other words, each person considers himself or herself the judge of whatever is true for him or her in any given circumstance.

Which model of truth do you sense your children or young people around you have accepted? In what way does this concern you or please you?

_____

_____

_____

_____

Someone read Deuteronomy 6:4-9, 20, and 24.

God's instructions for Israel are good for us today. What are some practical things each of us can do to instill a model of truth in our children that leads them from the precepts of the law to the person of the law? Identify two or three things you can do this week to model and instill a love for God and his ways into your children and family.

_____

_____

_____

_____

_____

_____

 Truth Encounter

Someone read Deuteronomy 10:12-13.

Why do you suspect it is sometimes hard to directly connect God's instructions to us to act a certain way to his loving heart, which gives them for our own good?

_____

_____

Someone read Psalm 119:18.

Before completing this exercise, pause and ask God to open your eyes to why he has given you his law. Ask to more clearly see God's heart.

_____

_____

_____

_____

Someone read Exodus 20:12.

There is a promise of provision that comes with this command.
What is it?

_____

_____

_____

_____

Someone read Exodus 20:15.

What is the command?

_____

_____

_____

Someone read Proverbs 2:7-8 and 11:3.

What is the promise of God's protection and provision for those
who are honest?

_____

_____

_____

_____

Someone read Exodus 20:17.

What is God's command?

_____

_____

Someone read 1 Timothy 6:6-10.

What is God's promise of protection for those who don't count riches?

_____

_____

_____

_____

Someone read Psalm 119:24.

Take turns verbalizing your gratitude for God's commands by completing the following sentence.

"I am glad God commanded us to _____
because I see his heart for my good. I am grateful because…

_____

_____

_____

_____."

Praise God for his loving heart to provide for us and protect us through obedience to his Word. Consider singing songs of praise and worship. Verbalize your praise in prayers of thanksgiving.

TruthTalk—An Assignment of the Week

This week share with a member of your family or friend what you have discovered in this session. Consider saying something like:

Being obedient to God's Word does not mean giving up the pleasures of leisure or satisfaction or liberty; it means being free to enjoy *maximum* leisure, *maximum* satisfaction, and *maximum* liberty—in the way God intended. God's prohibitions and directives to us come out of a heart of love that in effect says, "Follow in my ways and your joy

1 "In our small group we've been studying about God's Word, and I have gained a new view of his commands. I don't see them as just a list of things to do or not do. I see them as commands given for my good. For example…

_____
_____
_____
_____."

2 "I'm learning to now see God's heart behind some of the commands he's given us, and it's totally changing the way I see God and the Bible. For instance…

_____
_____

55

will be made complete." God always has our best interest at heart.

_____

_____."

3 "In our family, we follow the Bible. God tells us in the Bible that it is wrong to steal. He wants us to be honest. Can you think of some of the reasons why God tells us to be honest? Maybe, for instance…

_____

_____

_____

_____."

Read chapter 11 of *The Unshakable Truth* book.

Living Under God's Protection and Provision

Review: How did your TruthTalk assignment go this week? What was the response?

_____

_____

_____

_____

When you were growing up, did you have a different point of view than your parents on anything? What was it?

_____

_____

_____

_____

Every generation has some views different than those of their parents. But today that generation gap is wider than ever. A recent Pew Research Center study revealed that almost 80 percent of adults see a difference between the beliefs and points of view of young people and themselves. And the greatest difference is in the area of social values and morality.

What concerns you about the views on sexual morality of young people—yours or others close to you? Do you fear they may adopt the prevalent cultural view on sexual behavior? Comment.

_____

_____

_____

_____

_____

_____

_____

OUR GROUP OBJECTIVE

To gain a greater appreciation for why God wants us to be sexually moral and how to share that with our families.

How do we instill a biblical perspective on sexual morality into the next generation? First, we must model it before them. We must also teach them God's truth in the context of relationship.

Following is a group exercise that presents sexual morality in the context of relationship, demonstrating what God commands and why he commands it.

||||||||||||||||||||||||||||||||||||||||||||||||||||||||||||||||||||||||||||||||||||||||||||||||||||
God's Word on Sexual Immorality

How would you define sexual immorality?

_____

_____

_____

_____

Sexual immorality isn't limited to premarital sex. It is all sex that occurs outside of a marriage between one man and one woman (extramarital and premarital).

According to 1 Corinthians 6:18, what are we to flee or run away from? _____

According to 1 Corinthians 10:8, what are we to not engage in?

_____

According to Ephesians 5:3, what is improper for God's holy people? _____

According to 1 Thessalonians 4:3, in what way does God want us to be holy? By _____

_____

It is clear that God wants us to avoid sexual immorality.

‖‖

Why Is Sexual Immorality Wrong?

If all sin is a violation of God's character and nature, what is it about sexual immorality in particular that contradicts or goes against the image and likeness of God?

_____

_____

_____

_____

_____

There are at least two aspects of God's nature that sexual immorality violates.

‖‖

Reason #1

Someone read Exodus 20:5 and 34:14.

By nature God is a jealous God—his name is even called Jealous. What quality does this jealous nature reflect?

_____

_____

_____

_____

Someone read Deuteronomy 7:9.

What is the relationship between God's being jealous and faithful?

_____

_____

_____

_____

_____

Someone read the following:

> When Paul wrote that God wanted us to be holy
> and that we "should keep clear of all sexual sin"
> (1 Thessalonians 4:3) he was basing that command
> on the character and nature of a jealous God who
> wants fidelity, exclusivity, and faithfulness to him
> and only him. Sexual immorality violates human
> fidelity and exclusivity on every level.
>
> God wants our full and complete devotion. Because
> we were created in his image we want the exclusive
> love and devotion of one and only one person when
> it comes to sexual relations. Test yourself.

What if your spouse, or girlfriend or boyfriend, said this to you: "Out of the seven billion people alive today you are among the top five people I love dearly. Yes, you and four other people are the only ones I want to have sex with. You are that special." Now, would that make you feel truly special? Why or why not?

_____

_____

_____

_____

_____

To engage in premarital or extramarital sex is to connect with another in a way intended only for a committed marital relationship. It violates the very essence of exclusivity, oneness, and faithfulness of a love relationship, which is defined by the nature of God. That is one reason sexual immorality is wrong—it violates his faithful character.

||||||||||||||||||||||||||||||||||||||||||||||||||||||||||||||||||||||||||||||||||||||||||||||||||

Reason #2

Try this experiment. Lift up a glass or bottle of clear water. If the water is crystal clear you would say it is what? _____

Now drop a piece of dirt, stone, or any foreign object in the glass or bottle. You would now say the water is _____.

This experiment demonstrates that pure water is unadulterated—it is without a foreign object. When a foreign object enters the water it is adulterated—made unclean and impure.

What happens to the purity of a committed love relationship

when someone else enters it sexually? Why isn't that acceptable to you?

_____

_____

_____

_____

_____

Someone read 1 John 3:3 and Hebrews 13:4.

What character quality does 1 John indicate God is? _____

How is marriage honored according to this Hebrews passage?

_____

_____

_____

_____

To engage in sexual immorality dishonors the person you mar-
ried to the exclusion of all others—or will someday if you
choose to marry. It violates the nature of purity. God is pure,
and he wants the love relationship to be pure. That is another
reason premarital or extramarital sex is wrong.

||||||||||||||||||||||||||||||||||||||||||||||||||||||||||||||||||||||||||||||||||||||||||||||||

The Protection and Provision of Living in a Sexually Faithful and Pure Way

Think together of the negative consequences of unfaithfulness and impurity in a relationship and answer the questions below.

What are some possible consequences emotionally and relationally?

_____

_____

_____

_____

_____

What are some possible consequences physically (healthwise)?

_____

_____

_____

_____

What are some possible consequences spiritually?

_____

_____

_____

_____

What are some possible consequences reputation-wise?

_____

_____

_____

_____

What are some other possible consequences, if you can think of any?

_____

_____

_____

_____

_____

_____

_____

_____

Now from your list summarize God's protection.

||||||||||||||||||||||||||||||||||||||||||||||||||||||||||||||||||||||||||||

Living in a sexually moral way
protects us from:

- _____   - _____

- _____   - _____

- _____   - _____

Think together of the positive results of living in a sexually pure and faithful way in a relationship and respond below.

What are some positive results mentally and psychologically?

_____

_____

_____

_____

_____

What are some positive results spiritually?

_____

_____

_____

_____

_____

What are some positive results relationally?

_____

_____

_____

_____

_____

What are some positive results for a family?

_____

_____

_____

_____

_____

What are some other positive results?

_____

_____

_____

_____

_____

Now from your list summarize God's provision.

||||||||||||||||||||||||||||||||||||||||||||||||||||||||||||||||||||||||||||||||||||

Living in a sexually moral way provides the following things for us:

- _____   - _____

- _____   - _____

- _____   - _____

God gives us instructions for sexual morality in his Word because he wants us to reap the benefits of his protection and provision. He is honored when we live out his image of purity and faithfulness, and we are blessed.

Truth Encounter

Someone read Psalm 19:7.

Take time for two or more from the group to share the personal/emotional/relational rewards of their spouse's remaining pure and faithful to them. (Before proceeding with this exercise, be sensitive and discerning with individuals or couples who have experienced the painful consequences of a spouse or family member who has not been faithful.) As appropriate, celebrate together the joy of God's protection and provision.

_____

_____

_____

_____

_____

_____

Spend the next few moments sharing your gratitude and appreciation for how God wants to provide for us and protect us from the painful consequences of sexual impurity. Consider his faithfulness and his purity and how he deeply desires for us to emulate these characteristics so that we have the peace, security, and joy that he so wants for us. Consider singing songs of praise and worship.

_____

_____

_____

_____

_____

Truth Talk—An Assignment of the Week

This week take the time to sit down with a family member or friend and share how God provides and protects us when we obey his instructions to be sexually pure. Feel free to make copies of the pages of this session.

1 "I've been learning how God provides for us and protects us when we obey his instructions. For example, I am glad God has a specific standard for sexual purity. I know it sounds crazy, but I'm grateful he protects us from…

_____

and provides for…

_____

_____

God has given us his reliable Word that accurately reflects who he is (pure, faithful, a unity, and so on). Because he created us in his image, he provides instructions in his Word that show us how to conduct our lives in a way that reflects his nature. By following these instructions, we can live godly lives and enjoy the protection and provision he planned for us.

_____

_____."

2 "You know sex was God's idea and it can be very good. He _wants_ us to enjoy the terrific benefits of sex. God also wants to protect us from being robbed of those benefits. Here's what that means:

_____

_____

_____

_____."

3 "I've been learning how God is faithful. That means he is a perfect promise-keeper! He always does what he says, and he always remembers to keep his promises. I especially like that part of God's character because…

_____

_____

_____

_____."

Reread chapter 10, pages 115–116, in *The Unshakable Truth* to help you with your assignment, and also appendix B in preparation for the next session.

IIIIIIIIIIIIIIIIIIIIIIIIIIIIIIIIIIIIIIIIIIIIIIIIIIIIIIIIIIIIIIIIIIIIIIIIIIIIIIIIIIIIIIIIIIIIIIIIIIIII

Close in Prayer

CELEBRATING GOD'S WORD WITH YOUR FAMILY

Review: How did it go sharing with family or friend the protection and provision of God for being faithful and pure in marriage or dating? What was their response?

Someone read the following, drawn from appendix B of *The Unshakable Truth* book.

What Is the Revelation Celebration?

This is a family mealtime giving you as a group the opportunity to share the truth you have discovered about why God gave us his Word and the Holy Spirit, which reveal his truth to us.

The Revelation Celebration is designed as a Judeo-Christian family event that includes a meal. You will engage your children and teenagers in a fun and rewarding time illustrating that Scripture and the Holy Spirit are God's provisions to keep our relationships with him alive and fresh. The focus is on the ongoing process of coming to know God through his Word and the indwelling presence of the Holy Spirit.

This celebration is based on the Jewish holiday called the Festival of Harvest. In the Hebrew language of the Old Testament, it is called *Shavuot*. In the Greek language of the New Testament it is called *Pentecost*.

For centuries the Jewish people have gathered together in their homes to observe *Shavuot* by celebrating the revelation of God's written Word given to Moses on Mount Sinai. Scripture is God's revelation to us so we might know him and his ways. This is something to celebrate.

But there is something more to celebrate. The Holy Spirit was also given to us on the day of Pentecost to infill us and guide us into all truth. This Revelation Celebration is a time to celebrate God's revealed Word and the Holy Spirit, whom God sent as a means to know him on a deep relational level because he is the "God who is passionate about his relationship with you" (Exodus 34:14).

The Revelation Celebration is best done together with two

or more families. Children from three years of age and up will enjoy and get something out of this mealtime event. This session is a time to plan and go over the details and assign responsibilities for your celebration.

The celebration consists of six elements. Walk through each of these elements to practice and plan for your meal and the different readings. If your group is too large to fit into one home, plan to split up and conduct more than one celebration.

The six elements of the meal celebration do not include music, so your group may want to insert the singing of hymns or worship music at various times throughout the event.

1. *Identify an emcee/host.* Select someone in your group to be the emcee/host of the celebration the night of the meal. The guidelines for the emcee/host are found on pages 78–79.

2. *"Celebrating Two Revelations of God."* Identify someone in your group who is willing to read this presentation, which explains what the Revelation Celebration is all about. The reading is found on pages 80–81, and you have permission to photocopy those pages and all the pages related to this celebration. You might ask the person to read the material aloud to the group for practice using the

photocopied pages. We encourage you to *read* these readings at the celebration meal rather than casually relating the content. The exception is "The Verbal Relay Process" illustration.

3. *"Why We Celebrate."* Identify someone within your group who is willing to read this presentation, found on pages 82–87. Ask him or her to read it aloud now to familiarize everyone with the material.

4. *The meal.* Identify someone in your group who is willing to take the lead to coordinate the location of the Revelation Celebration (preferably someone's home), identify the time, obtain the prescribed menu items, determine what else is served, and so on.

   This person is not to do all the work. He or she is to work with group members to coordinate the logistical details of the celebration, listed on page 88. Photocopy that page and provide it to the meal coordinator.

5. *"The Verbal Relay Process."* Identify someone in your group who is willing to conduct this illustration, found on pages 89–92. Make a

photocopy of those pages and ask him or her to read it aloud to familiarize everyone with the illustration.

6. *"God's Accurate Letters of Love."* Identify some-one who is willing to read this information, found on pages 93–98. Ask him or her to read these pages aloud now to familiarize the group with this material.

7. *"From God's Heart to Yours."* Identify someone within your group who is willing to read this presentation, found on pages 99–103. Ask him or her to read it aloud now to familiarize everyone with its content.

||||||||||||||||||||||||||||||||||||||||||||||||||||||||||||||||||||||||||||||||||||||||||||||

Conducting the Revelation Celebration

After meeting with the families you plan to have the Revelation Celebration with, you are now ready to emcee your evening event and meal. Photocopy these pages as a reference guide to your actual celebration.

- *Introduction*: Invite everyone to be seated at the table and say, **"Tonight we are going to have a celebration and _____ (name) is going to start us off"** ("Celebrating Two Revelations of God").

- Immediately following that presentation have the person responsible for the "Why We Celebrate" make his or her presentation.

- Announcement of the meal and the prayer for the meal will be given by the person presenting "Why We Celebrate."

- At the conclusion of the meal, thank all those who helped prepare it. Then say, **"Now _____ (name) has something to share with us"** ("The Verbal Relay Process").

- After the verbal relay presentation say, **"Now, to see how accurate the lifesaving message of**

the Bible is, let's have _____ (name) **read something very fascinating, entitled 'God's Accurate Letters of Love.'"**

- Following that presentation, after a moment of silence, share from your own heart how you desire to know God more through his Spirit and his Word. Encourage others to share their desires to know God more. After a time of sharing consider singing a worship song and then close in prayer.

Celebrating Two Revelations of God

Tonight we are going to participate in what we are calling the "Revelation Celebration." It is based on a Jewish holiday. The Jewish holiday is called the Festival of Harvest. In the Greek language of the New Testament it is called *Pentecost*.

For centuries the Jewish people gathered together in their homes and observed the Festival of Harvest by celebrating the revelation of God's written Word given to Moses on Mount Sinai. God appeared to Moses and said, "I am the LORD, the merciful and gracious God. I am slow to anger and rich in unfailing love…You must worship no other gods, but only the LORD, for he is a God who is passionate about his relationship with you" (Exodus 34:6,14).

God gave the children of Israel and each of us his Word as his love letters on how to come to know him personally. Because humans have sinned against him, they are separated from him. The Scriptures—his written Word—are instructions on how to regain a personal love relationship with him.

Tonight we will celebrate God's revealing himself to us through his holy Word so we can know him for who he is.

Hundreds of years after Moses, it was written in Scripture that "the Word became human and lived here on earth among us" (John 1:14). His name was Jesus. He told his followers that to redeem them he must die for their sins, but that he would rise from the dead. He also said, "I will ask the Father, and he will give you another Counselor, who will never leave you. He is the Holy Spirit, who leads into all truth" (John 14:16). And the Bible says that "God has actually given us his Spirit…so we can know the wonderful things God has freely given us" (1 Corinthians 2:12).

During the Jewish Passover celebration, Jesus was, in fact, crucified. But just as he had said, he rose again and went back to his Father God in heaven. And 50 days from the Passover, when the Festival of Harvest, or Pentecost, was observed by the Jewish people, something extraordinary happened—just as Jesus had promised. It is recorded in the second chapter of Acts.

> On the day of Pentecost, seven weeks after Jesus' resurrection, the believers were meeting together in one place. Suddenly, there was a sound from heaven like the roaring of a mighty windstorm in the skies above them, and it filled the house where they were meeting. Then, what looked like flames or tongues of fire appeared and settled on each of them. And every one present was filled with the Holy Spirit (Acts 2:1-4).

We too will celebrate God's revealing himself to us by giving us his Holy Spirit.

So tonight we celebrate God's revelation of his Word. Tonight we celebrate God's revelation of his Holy Spirit.

Why We Celebrate

Instructions: At the end of this reading there are three group readings to photocopy, cut out, and distribute to three young people who will be attending your Revelation Celebration. Pull them aside and ask them to help you out with your reading. They are simply to read aloud what is written, on your cue.

Also ask the youngest child who can speak and will be attending the celebration to assist you. Ask the child to simply say, "Because," when you nod at him or her. This child will need to be able to be attentive to your reading and cues.

You will need a cluster of grapes as an object lesson and enough small clusters to give to each person at the Revelation Celebration meal. Be sure the cluster you use has a main vine clearly visible, from which numerous grapes extend.

Read aloud:

"Why do we celebrate tonight? We celebrate because God has revealed himself through the written Word and through his Holy Spirit. But what does that really mean to us?

"God's revelation through his written Word and through his Holy Spirit means everything to you and me, because the Spirit and the Word teach and empower us to accomplish the one thing we were meant to accomplish—and that is to enjoy relationships. We were created to revel in a love relationship with God and with one another because, as Exodus 34:14 says, 'He is a God who is passionate about his relationship with you.'

"I have asked _____ (name of youngest child) to assist me. Each time (he or she) says, "Because," I would like all of you to quote that scripture aloud in unison: 'He is a God who is passionate about his relationship with you.' Okay?"

> **"Why did God give you his written Word?"**
> (Nod to youngest child to say, "Because.")
> (**Group says in unison,** "He is a God who is passionate about his relationship with you.") [Repeat this again if the group is unclear what they were to do.]
>
> **"Why did God give you his Holy Spirit?"**
> (Nod to youngest child to say, "Because.")
> (**Group says in unison,** "He is a God who is passionate about his relationship with you.")
>
> **"Why did God create you to love him and one another?"** (Nod to youngest child to say, "Because.")
> (**Group says in unison,** "He is a God who is passionate about his relationship with you.")

Now nod to the teenager/young person to whom you gave Reading #1 to indicate that he or she is to read it aloud. *Note:* As previously mentioned, before your meal event make a photocopy of all three of these readings and cut them out so you can give one to each person doing the reading.

(photocopy and cut here)

READING #1

We celebrate the revelation of your Holy Word, O God, for it allows us to know you for who you are. You said to Moses as recorded in Exodus 33, "I know you by name, and I'm pleased with you." And Moses replied, "If you're really pleased with me, show me your ways so I can know you." Your Holy Word reveals yourself and your ways to us. We celebrate the giving of your Holy Word tonight.

Nod to the teenager/young person with Reading #2 to indicate that he or she is to read it aloud.

(photocopy and cut here)

READING #2

We celebrate the revealing of your Holy Spirit, O God, on the day of Pentecost, for you have come to fill us not only with your Word, but with your presence also. You desire for us to join you in the circle of your perfect relationship. You said, "My prayer for all of them is that they will be one, just as you and I are one, Father—that just as you are in me and I am in you, so they will be in us" (John 17:21). Your Holy Spirit has come to indwell us and make us one with you. We celebrate the giving of your Holy Spirit tonight.

Nod to the teenager/young person with Reading #3 to indicate that he or she is to read it aloud.

(photocopy and cut here)

READING #3

Tonight we celebrate the revelation of your Spirit and your Word. And in doing so we celebrate how your love toward us and in us has enabled us to love one another as you have loved us. You said to your followers as recorded in John 13, "Love each other in the same way that I have loved you. Everyone will know that you are my disciples because of your love for each other." Your Spirit and your Word enable us to truly love as you love. We celebrate our love for one another tonight.

Pick up the cluster of grapes. Ask each person to take a small bunch from those that you have provided on a tray, and say the following:

"Jesus said, 'I am the vine; you are the branches. Those who remain in me, and I in them, will produce much fruit. For apart from me you can do nothing' (John 15:5).

"Christ is the vine. We are the branches. This grape represents the fruit of his love. When we yield to God's Holy Word and the Holy Spirit living in us, we produce the fruit of Christlike loving. Each of you now take the fruit of the vine and eat it." (You pick a grape from the cluster and eat it as well.)

"Tonight we celebrate his love and our love for one another. Right now let someone know that you love him or her." (To set an example, you go over and embrace someone and say, "I love you." Once everyone has expressed a gesture of love to another, say the following:)

"Now, because of God's revelation of his Spirit and his Word, we celebrate him and our love for one another. And how do we do that? For one, by feasting!" (If you decide to sing, say:) **"By singing and feasting."** (Then lead in a song. Now offer the following prayer:)

"O God, we celebrate your Spirit and the Word tonight. We celebrate our love for one another. And as we partake of this food, bless it so that it strengthens us to honor you by loving one another as you have loved us. Amen."

Serve the meal.

||||||||||||||||||||||||||||||||||||||||||||||||||||||||||||||||||||||||||||||||||||||

The Meal Surrounding
Our Celebration

- *Select where to conduct your Revelation Celebration.* A person's home is preferable, depending on the size of your group and their families. Conducting the celebration simultaneously at multiple sites is an option if you have a large group.

- *Select the date and time of your celebration.*

- *Decide on the meal.* Consider a potluck meal in which each family brings a dish. This time together is a time of feasting. Decide who in your group will bring what. As an object lesson you will need to have a large cluster of grapes at your celebration meal. Be sure that at least part of the cluster you use has a main vine clearly visible, from which numerous small bunches extend.

The Verbal Relay Process

Instructions: Prior to your celebration event write or type five labels to be placed on five small paper cups. The five labels should read, "Hyprochloric Acid," "Hygrochloric Acid," "Hylochloric Acid," "Hyfrochloric Acid," and "Hydrochloric Acid." Then put one candy mint in each cup. Also write or type the words "A Hyfrochloric Acid Pill" on a small slip of paper and fold it once to hide the wording. Then place the five cups on a tray and put the slip of paper in your pocket.

Presentation

(familiarize yourself with this illustration so you don't need to read from the presentation):

Say: **"I need the help of** _____
(name—choose a young person ten or older in your group)
and _____ (name—an adult) **to help
me.** _____ (name of young person),
you are a medical doctor with, among other things, this medication (provide the tray with the five cups of mints).

"_____ (name of adult), **you have
a fatal and rare disease called *'melodrama fatalis'* that can
be cured by only one of these pills. I know the name of that**

pill and will pass it on to our fine doctor here through a verbal relay process. (Ask your young doctor to come to where you are standing). **"But I will relay the name of that all-important pill to** _____ (name of the person seated closest to you) **only once and ask him or her to whisper it to the person beside him or her only once. Then he or she must whisper it to the next and the next, each person saying it only once, until it is finally whispered to our fine doctor here. Now time is of the essence, so let's get this verbal relay going as quickly as possible. Remember, you can whisper what you hear only once. And of course, you cannot ask the previous person to repeat what was whispered—and we must move fast because our patient is dying."**

(Whisper "Hyfrochloric Acid Pill" to the person next to you and get the relay going. Once the information has traveled around the table to the last person near you and your doctor, ask the person to whisper the pill's name to the doctor. Then facing your young doctor say:)

"Now what is the word that was whispered in your ear?" (After he or she has replied by repeating the word whispered to him or her, show your doctor friend the five labeled paper cups and have him or her again repeat the name he or she heard whispered. The name heard will undoubtedly be jumbled and unlike any of the specific labeled names. Say:) **"None of these pills match the name you said, so you must take a**

chance." (Let the doctor choose the cup bearing the name closest to what he or she heard. Then say:) **"Since this is your best guess as to the right pill, go ahead and take the chance; give this pill to our dying friend."** (Ask the adult to eat the pill. Then hand the folded slip of paper to the doctor from your pocket and ask him or her to read it. Then say:)

"Does it match the pill _____ **(name** of adult) **took?"** (It most likely won't. Even if it does, point out it was simply a shot in the dark and that it was an unlikely miracle the patient was saved. However, in all likelihood the right pill was not chosen. Say to the adult:) **"You are out of luck. You took the wrong pill, and so you must now 'pass away.'"** (The more the adult hams this up, the better. Then say:)

"Let me ask all of you: What went wrong with this verbal relay process of getting the name of the cure to our expert doctor?" (Let the group respond. All will agree the message got garbled in the process of transmission.)

"Right. Doctor _____ (name of young volunteer) **had no way to be sure he or she was giving poor** _____ (name of adult) **the correct remedy because the vital information he needed was distorted along the way. Without accurate, undistorted instructions, our dying patient couldn't experience the lifesaving power of that information.**

"Now, what does this illustration tell us about those who copied the Bible by hand generation after generation?" (Wait for a response. Lead the group to the conclusion that the words of Scripture had to be passed down accurately. Then say:)

"That's right. If we are to read the exact lifesaving words God gave to those who first wrote them down, then those copying Scripture had to be careful to copy accurately, letter for letter, word for word."

The emcee thanks the person for conducting the illustration and says: **"Now, to see how accurate the lifesaving message of the Bible is, let's have** _____ (name of adult) **read something very fascinating, entitled 'God's Accurate Letters of Love.'"**

God's Accurate Letters of Love

(Make copies for everyone to read along.)

God spoke to men thousands of years ago and had them write down very important messages he wanted us to know. Because he loved us and wanted a relationship with us, he wanted us to know how we could get to know him. All of us as humans had sinned and were separated from him, so his Word was to become our instructions, or set of love letters from God, on how to come to know him personally.

Do we have an accurate set of love letters? Were the copies made of the original writings done accurately? Let's find out.

The case of the meticulous scribes

Hand-copying of the Old Testament was the responsibility of a group of men who were trained as skilled scribes and gave their lives to writing. For many years before and after the time of Jesus it was their responsibility to copy Scripture. These particular scribes, some known as Masoretic scribes, devoted themselves to making sure that the Holy Scriptures were copied letter for letter, word for word. Their rules for copying Scripture were so strict that when a copy was made it was considered to be an exact duplicate, just as if you had made it from a copy machine. When a copy was finished it was called a manuscript.

A scribe would begin his day of transcribing a manuscript by ceremonially washing his entire body. He would then robe himself in full Jewish dress before sitting down at his desk. As he wrote, if he came to the Hebrew name of God, he could not begin writing the name with a pen newly dipped in ink for fear it would smear the page. Once he began writing the name of God, he could not stop or allow himself to be distracted…even if a king were to enter the room. The scribe was obligated to continue without interruption until he finished penning the holy name of the one true God.

The Masoretic guidelines for copying manuscripts also required that

- the scroll be written on the skin of a clean animal.

- each skin contain a specified number of columns, equal throughout the entire book.

- the length of each column extend no less than 48 lines and no more than 60.

- the column breadth consist of exactly 30 letters.

- the space of a thread appear between every consonant.

- the breadth of nine consonants be inserted between each section.

- a space of three lines appear between each book.

- the fifth book of Moses (Deuteronomy) conclude exactly with a full line.

- nothing—not even the shortest word—be copied from memory, but rather be copied letter by letter.

- the scribe count the number of times each letter of the alphabet occurred in each book and compare it to the original.

- if a manuscript was found to contain even one mistake, it be discarded.

God instilled in the Masoretes such a painstaking reverence for the Hebrew Scriptures in order to ensure the amazingly accurate transmission of the Bible, so you and I would have an accurate revelation of him.

The case of the accurate New Testament

The Hebrew scribes did not copy the manuscripts of the New Testament. So God did a new thing to ensure that the words of Jesus and his followers would be preserved accurately for us.

To tell if ancient manuscripts are reliable we 1) measure the time between the original writing and the first manuscript copy; and 2) determine how many manuscript copies are still in existence. The shorter the time between the original writing and the first copy and the more manuscripts there are, the more accurate the manuscripts are considered.

For example, virtually everything we know today about Julius Caesar's campaigns in Gaul (present-day France) comes from ten manuscript copies of *The Gallic Wars*, the earliest of which dates to just within 1000 years of the time it was originally written. The most reliable writing in secular history is Homer's *Iliad,* with 643 manuscripts, the earliest of which dates to within 400 years of the original writing.

Let's look at this chart of classical literature.

Author	Book	Date written	Date of earliest existing copies	Time gap	Number of copies
Homer	*Iliad*	800 BC	c. 400 BC	c. 400 years	643
Herodotus	*History*	480–425 BC	c. AD 900	c. 1350 years	8
Thucydides	*History*	460–400 BC	AD 900	c. 1300 years	8
Plato		400 BC	c. AD 900	c. 1300 years	7
Demosthenes		300 BC	c. AD 1100	c. 1400 years	200
Caesar	*Gallic Wars*	100–44 BC	c. AD 900	c. 1000 years	10
Livy	*History of Rome*	59 BC–AD 17	fourth century (partial); mostly tenth century	c. 400 years c. 1000 years	1 partial 19 complete
Tacitus	*Annals*	AD 100	c. AD 1100	c. 1000 years	20
Pliny Secundus	*Natural History*	AD 61–113	c. AD 850	c. 750 years	7

II

The New Testament has no equal

Using this accepted standard for evaluating the reliability of ancient writings, the New Testament stands alone. It has no equal. No other book of the ancient world can even compare to its reliability. Take a look at this chart:

Author	Book	Date of earliest existing copies	Time gap	Number of copies
John	New Testament	c. AD 130	50-plus years	Fragments
The rest of the New Testament books		c. AD 200 (books)	100 years	
		c. AD 250 (most of New Testament)	150 years	
		c. AD 325 (complete New Testament)	225 years	5600-plus Greek manuscripts
		c. AD 366–384 (Latin Vulgate translation)	284 years	
		c. AD 400–500 (other transla-tions)	400 years	19,000-plus translated manuscripts
		TOTALS	50-400 years	24,900-plus manuscripts

There are nearly 25,000 manuscripts or fragments of manu-scripts, with some dating back to within 50 years of the original writings. And none are more than 400 years more recent than the originals. Incredible!

When you hold a Bible in your hand you can be sure it is the most accurate and reliable writing in all of history! God wanted you to be sure that the Bible you read is the accurate love letters he had written just for you.

‖‖

From God's Heart to Yours

Instructions: Practice reading this presentation until you can read it with passion and feeling. It is designed to help those at your celebration capture God's heart for personal relationship.

‖‖

Say:

"I am going to read something as though God is personally sharing his heart with us tonight."

I am the Alpha and the Omega, the beginning and the end. I am the one who is, who always was, and who is still to come, the Almighty One.

I am the infinite God who knows no boundaries or limitations. My power and knowledge and greatness are beyond your comprehension. My love and holiness and beauty are so intense that for you to see me in all my glory would overwhelm you— for as a mortal you could not see me and live. And yet…I created you to know me intimately, for I am passionate about my relationship with you.

But a relationship isn't complete unless the love cycle—each one of us knowing and being known— is completed. I want you to know that I know you, and I want you to know me.

I know everything there is to know about you. I know your favorite color, your favorite food, what music you like, the dreams you have, and the future you long for. I know your struggles and weaknesses. I am glad with you when you make right choices. I am saddened when you make wrong choices. I know you better than you know yourself, and…I love you.

But I want to ask you a question—not for my information, but for yours. Do you love me? I mean *really* love me? Be slow to answer; be sure before you speak. And before you do, let me tell you the secret to really loving me. To love me, you must come to know me. For to know me is to love me!

Learn of my mercy and my faithfulness, and you will love me. Come to know my goodness and holiness, and you will love me. Learn of my justice tempered with patience, and you will love me. Know what I love and what I hate, and you will love me. Know what saddens my heart and what gives me pleasure, and you will love me.

This is the way to have eternal life: to know me, the only true God. And the more you know me, the more you will become like me. The more you know me, the more you will praise and thank me and honor my name. And the more you know me, the more you will love others as I love them.

There are two ways to know me. The first is through my Holy Spirit. I have sent you my Spirit to live within you. Allow me to fill you with my Spirit. Make me at home in your heart. Speak to me often in your prayers. Confide your fears, your hopes, your dreams to me. Let me live my life through you. I am with you always, and I will never leave you.

The second way to know me is through the written revelation of me—my Holy Word, the collection of my love letters to you. Read my words, hide them in your heart, and know me for who I am—the one true God, your Savior, and your friend.

I long for you to communicate with me by opening your heart in prayer. As you hear the words of the following prayer, I urge you to make the prayer your own, and let the words come from your heart. Pray silently to me:

> Oh, God, you are great, but I know so little of your greatness. I know you are merciful and faithful and holy and just, but I really know so little of you.

> I want to thank you for your Holy Spirit. I welcome you to be more and more at home in my heart. And I thank you for your Holy Word and for giving to me right now, this

very moment, a longing to know you and a
hunger to read your love letters to me.

I ask you to help me. Help me by giving me
a desire to read your Word more often. As
I read, help me to see you and know you in
every page, so I can be like you. Oh, God,
let me honor you with my life. I sense you
smiling at me right now. Thank you. Thank
you for loving me. I love you too. Amen.

Emcee: After a moment of silence, share from your own heart
how you desire to know God more through his Spirit and his
Word. Encourage others to share their desires to know God
more. After a time of sharing, consider singing a worship song.

||||||||||||||||||||||||||||||||||||||||||||||||||||||||||||||||||||||||||||||||||||||||||||

*Consider reading this prayer at the end
of the celebration:*

"Tonight, O Lord, we have celebrated the revelation of your
Holy Word and the revelation of your Holy Spirit. You have
given us your Spirit and your Word that we might know you
and love you intimately. And in doing so you have enabled
us to love our wives and husbands, mothers and fathers, sons
and daughters, grandparents, grandchildren, and friends as
you meant for us to love them—with Christlike, unselfish love.

"Help us to go away from this celebration more lovingly committed to you and to one another. And let this prayer from your apostle Paul in Ephesians 3 be our concluding prayer:

> I pray that from his glorious, unlimited resources
> he will give you mighty inner strength through his
> Holy Spirit. And I pray that Christ will be more and
> more at home in your hearts as you trust in him.
> May your roots go down deep into the soil of God's
> marvelous love. And may you have the power to
> understand, as all God's people should, how wide,
> how long, how high, and how deep his love really
> is. May you experience the love of Christ, though
> it is so great you will never fully understand it.
> Then you will be filled with the fullness of life and
> power that comes from God. Now glory be to
> God! By his mighty power at work within us, he is
> able to accomplish infinitely more than we would
> ever dare to ask or hope. May he be given glory
> in the church and in Christ Jesus forever and ever
> through endless ages. Amen (verses 16-21).

"And everyone said...Amen!"

Take the Complete Unshakable Truth® Journey!

The Unshakable Truth Journey gets to the heart of what being a true follower of Christ means and what knowing him is all about. Each five-session course is based one of 12 core truths of the Christian faith presented in Josh and Sean McDowell's book *The Unshakable Truth®*.

The Unshakable Truth Journey is uniquely positioned for today's culture because it 1) highlights how Christianity's beliefs affect relationships, 2) promotes a relational, group context in which Christians can experience the teaching in depth, and 3) shows believers how they can live out Christianity's central truths before their community and world.

More than just a program, The Unshakable Truth Journey is a tool for long-term change and transformation!

CREATED—EXPERIENCE YOUR UNIQUE PURPOSE is devoted to the truth that God is—he exists, and he created human beings for a reason. It lays a foundation for who people are because they're God's creation, who God designed them to be, and how they can live a life of fulfillment.

INSPIRED—EXPERIENCE THE POWER OF GOD'S WORD explores the truth that God has spoken and revealed himself to humanity within the Bible. Further, he gave us his Word for a very clear purpose—to provide for us and protect us.

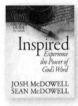

BROKEN—EXPERIENCE VICTORY OVER SIN examines the truth about humankind's brokenness because of original sin, humankind's ongoing problem with sin, and how instead to make right choices in life.

ACCEPTED—EXPERIENCE GOD'S UNCONDITIONAL LOVE opens up the truth about God's redemption plan. The truth that God became human establishes his unconditional acceptance of us, which defines our worth. God values us in spite of our sin. This is the basis on which we gain a high sense of worth.

SACRIFICE—EXPERIENCE A DEEPER WAY TO LOVE digs into the truth about Christ's atonement. The truth that Christ had to die to purchase our salvation shows the true meaning of love—and how God can bring us into a right relationship with him in spite of our sin.

FORGIVEN—EXPERIENCE THE SURPRISING GRACE OF GOD explores the truth about the power of God's grace. The truth that God can offer us forgiveness in spite of our sin helps us understand how we actually obtain a relationship with him.

GROWING—EXPERIENCE THE DYNAMIC PATH TO TRANSFORMATION speaks to the truth about our transformed life in Christ. The truth about our transformed life in Christ defines who we are in this world and shows how we can know our purpose in life.

RESURRECTED—EXPERIENCE FREEDOM FROM THE FEAR OF DEATH focuses on the truth about Christ's resurrection. The truth that Christ rose from the grave and that his resurrection is a historical event assures us of eternal life and overcomes any fear of dying.

EMPOWERED—EXPERIENCE LIVING IN THE POWER OF THE SPIRIT covers the truth about the Trinity. The truth that God is three in one and defines how relationships work through the Holy Spirit lays the foundation for how we can experience the power of the Spirit.

PERSPECTIVE—EXPERIENCE THE WORLD THROUGH GOD'S EYES examines the truth about God's kingdom and how it defines a biblical worldview. These sessions show how to gain a biblical worldview.

COMMUNITY—EXPERIENCE JESUS ALIVE IN HIS PEOPLE opens up the truth about the church. The truth about Christ's body—the church—provides us with our mission in life and shows us how to experience true community.

RESTORED—EXPERIENCE THE JOY OF YOUR DESTINY is devoted to the truth about the return of Christ. The truth that Jesus is coming back helps us grasp our destiny in life and gain an eternal perspective on life and death.

The Unshakable Truth Journey
Inspired Growth Guide Evaluation Form

1. How many on average participated in your group? _____

2. Did you read all or a portion of *The Unshakable Truth* book? _____

3. Did your group leader use visual illustrations during this course? _____

4. *Group leader:* Was your experience connecting to the web and viewing the video illustrations acceptable? Explain.

   _____

   _____

5. On a scale of 1 to 10 (10 being the highest) how would you rate:

   a) the quality and usefulness of the session content? _____
   b) the responsiveness and interaction of those in your group? _____

6. To what degree did this course deepen your practical understanding of the truths it covered?

   ❑ Little   ❑ Somewhat   ❑ Rather considerably

   Please give any comments you feel would be helpful to us.

   _____

   _____

   _____

   _____

Please mail to: Josh McDowell Evaluation
                 PO Box 4126
                 Copley, OH 44321

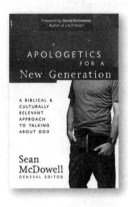

The Awesome Book of Bible Answers for Kids

Josh McDowell and Kevin Johnson

These concise, welcoming answers include key Bible verses and explorations of topics that matter most to kids ages 8 to 12: God's love; right and wrong; Jesus, the Holy Spirit, and God's Word; different beliefs and religions; church, prayer, and sharing faith. Josh and Kevin look at questions like...

- How do I know God wants to be my friend?

- Are parts of the Bible make-believe, or is everything true?

- Was Jesus a wimp?

- Why do some Christians not act like Christians?

- Can God make bad things turn out okay?

The next time a child in your life asks a good question, this practical and engaging volume will give you helpful tips and conversation ideas so you can connect with them and offer straight talk about faith in Jesus. *Includes an easy-to-use learning and conversation guide.*

The Unshakable Truth® church and small group resource collections are part of a unique collaboration between Harvest House Publishers and the Great Commandment Network. The Great Commandment Network is an international network of denominational partners, churches, parachurch ministries and strategic ministry leaders who are committed to the development of ongoing Great Commandment ministries worldwide as they prioritize the powerful simplicity of loving God, loving others and making disciples.

Through accredited trainers, the Great Commandment Network equips churches for ongoing relational ministry utilizing resources from the GC² Experience collection.

The GC² Experience Vision

To provide process-driven resources for a lifelong journey of spiritual formation. Every resource includes intentional opportunities to live out life-changing content within the context of loving God, loving others, and making disciples (Matthew 22:37-40; 28:19-20).

The GC² Experience Process includes:

- Experiential and transformative content. People are relationally transformed when they encounter Jesus, experience his Word, and engage in authentic community.

- Opportunities to move through a journey of…

  - Exploring Truth in the safety of relationship
  - Embracing Truth in a personal way
  - Experiencing Truth in everyday life
  - Expressing Truth through my identity as a Christ-follower

"Most of us have attended too many meetings and have gone through too many courses, only to conclude: We're leaving unchanged, and the people in our lives can see that we're unchanged. It is time to trust God for something different…a movement of life-changing transformation!"

Dr. David Ferguson
The Great Commandment Network

The Transforming Promise of Great Commandment/Great Commission Living
www.GC2experience.com